new life in
CHRIST

steve pettit

new life in
CHRIST

A Study in Ephesians

journey**forth**®

Greenville, South Carolina

The fact that materials produced by other publishers may be referred to in this volume does not constitute an endorsement of the content or theological position of materials produced by such publishers.

All Scripture is quoted from the King James Version.

Photo credits: Steve Pettit © 2016, Hal Cook, BJU Marketing Communications

Contributor: Eric Newton
Art Director: Elly Kalagayan
Designer: Matthew Freeland
Page layout: Michael Boone

ISBN 978-1-62856-059-6
eISBN 978-1-62856-381-8

15 14 13 12 11 10 9 8 7 6 5 4 3 2 1

Contents

KEY

Personal Application

Group Discussion

Cross Reference

Word Definition

Study Tip

01
Introduction to Ephesians

What is the most impressive thing you have ever seen? Was it an amazing view of a mountain or an ocean or ancient ruins? Perhaps a remarkable feat of human skill or endurance? Because of our affluence and technology, we have the capability to view photography and explore regions and enjoy experiences that are truly astounding.

But what about the angels? What about those who minister in the immediate presence of God and have a front row seat for all His works? What is most impressive to them? This may initially seem like an unanswerable question. However, Paul tells us in Ephesians 3:10 that by the preaching of the gospel God is working so that "now unto the principalities and powers in heavenly places might be known by the church the manifold wisdom of God." In other words, God the Father is doing something for His Son in the church by His Spirit for His own glory that astonishes the angels. Paul's letter to the Ephesians declares this glory and directs our response.

In order to understand the background of our study, we will answer four questions in our first two chapters.

1. Where did Paul's original audience live?
2. How did the Ephesian church begin?
3. Why did Paul write this letter?
4. What are the letter's major themes?

The City

Ephesus was a very important city for multiple reasons. First, it was a highly populated city. At the time this epistle was written, Ephesus was the fourth largest city in the western world (behind Rome; Alexandria, Egypt; and Antioch, Syria respectively), boasting a population of approximately 250,000 people. Second, Ephesus was important for political reasons. It served as the capital of the Roman province of Asia (essentially, what is now Turkey).

Third, Ephesus stood out because of religion. The primary reason for this prominence was its temple. Located in the heart of the city, the Temple of Diana (whom the Greeks called Artemis) was one of the Seven Wonders of the Ancient World. Probably the largest building in the world at that time, its massive size measured two hundred feet wide by four hundred feet long. It boasted 127 columns (many overlaid with gold) standing sixty feet tall to support the roof. An annual festival for the goddess Diana brought in up to half a million worshipers each year.

One biblical evidence of Ephesus's false religion was the inhabitants' response to Paul's miracles and preaching. The Ephesians burned so many books about magic that the value was equivalent to nearly 140 years' pay for an ordinary laborer (Acts 19:19). This renunciation of superstitious idol worship was endangering the local economy and, therefore, the magnificence of Diana and the significance of Ephesus (Acts 19:27). The silversmith Demetrius felt so strongly about this turn of events caused by Paul's influence on the city that he incited a riot (Acts 19:24–25).

The Church

Paul came to Ephesus on his way to Jerusalem at the end of his second missionary journey. After his first visit he left a godly couple, Priscilla and Aquila, with the Ephesians (Acts 18:18–21). They were responsible for helping the gifted Apollos by "expound[ing] unto him the way of God more perfectly" (18:26), so that his understanding of Christian baptism went beyond John's baptism of repentance (18:25). Paul later returned and stayed well over two years teaching and preaching the gospel (19:10).

The accounts in Acts open a window into the early Ephesian church. There was clearly more Jewish influence in this church than in some other churches the apostle started and later wrote letters to (for example, Philippi). During his time there, Paul taught some disciples of John the Baptist the way of salvation in Christ, and they received the Holy Spirit (19:1–7). In addition, Paul spoke in the Ephesian synagogue for three months, "disputing and persuading the things concerning the kingdom of God" (19:8). When mounting Jewish resistance signaled it was time for Paul to cease proclaiming God's kingdom in the synagogue, "he departed from them and separated the disciples" (19:9). These disciples undoubtedly had a solidly Jewish background.

Paul went next door to "disput[e] daily in the school of one Tyrannus" (19:9). Though this move did not mean the end of Jewish evangelism in Ephesus, clearly his focus had shifted to Gentiles. In fact, the effects of his teaching ministry were astounding: "all they which dwelt in Asia heard the word of the Lord Jesus, both Jews and Greeks" (19:10). The growing number of Gentiles who were forsaking their pagan spirituality and believing the apostolic gospel (19:18–19) provoked the outrage and riotous leadership of Demetrius (19:24–32). Luke comments, "So mightily grew the word of God and prevailed" (19:20).

The Ephesian church continued to be significant throughout the first century. After Paul's departure, Timothy became the pastor and stayed there for many years. But Paul continued to care deeply about this church. He shared an emotional farewell with the Ephesian elders on his return trip to Jerusalem (20:17–38). Later, while imprisoned in Rome, Paul wrote to Timothy in Ephesus, not just once (1 Tim. 1:3) but twice (2 Tim. 1:18). According to church history the apostle John later pastored in Ephesus. Nearly four decades after Christ initially began building His church in Ephesus, its members received the book of Revelation (Rev. 2:1) and probably John's letters too.

The Letter

Paul wrote this epistle while imprisoned in the city of Rome between AD 60 and 62. Since he does not explicitly address specific problems in his letter, this was probably a circular letter written for and distributed to all believers and churches around the city of Ephesus.

Of the twenty-one New Testament epistles, only Ephesians focuses on God the Father as the primary subject of the letter; all the rest make God the Son the subject. Paul reveals that the Father is preparing a bride for His Son, Jesus Christ. This body, called *the church*, is made up of believing Jews and Gentiles. In explaining this, Paul unfolds a great mystery hidden in times past, but now revealed to the Gentiles. God has broken down the division that existed between these two groups and created a new humanity (the church), where Jews and Gentiles live together in unity through Jesus Christ.

God designated two religious groups of people in the world: Jews and Gentiles. *Gentile* was a name given by God to the nations that were separated by God at the tower of Babel (Gen. 10). The Jews originated from the family of Abraham. God's covenant with this patriarch guaranteed that Abraham's family would be blessed and would become a great nation. One distinguishing characteristic of the Jews was the circumcision of all males as a sign of God's covenant with His chosen people. God describes the Gentiles as being *heathen*. (Lev. 26:33, for example) This term later came to mean *irreligious, unenlightened*, and in many cases, *savage*. Paul uses the term *Gentiles* to refer to those who are without Christ, spiritually dead because of their sins (Eph. 2:1) and enslaved to lustful desires (2:2–3).

Since Christ's coming to earth, many Gentiles have experienced a spiritual conversion. They have been made alive in Christ and raised from spiritual death (2:5–6). They experience a relationship with God through the blood of Christ (2:13) and are now citizens of God's kingdom and members of God's family (2:19). Therefore, all believers are called to live worthy of this new life by being different from the unconverted Gentiles (4:1, 17).

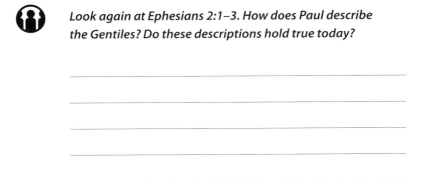

Look again at Ephesians 2:1–3. How does Paul describe the Gentiles? Do these descriptions hold true today?

Conclusion

Paul wrote this letter to a group of churches near a prominent city in the Roman Empire. The church in Ephesus consisted of both Jews and Gentiles, who faced understandable challenges in being unified with one another as well as distinct from their godless culture. Therefore, the Holy Spirit guides Paul to write a letter full of rich theology and practical application.

To understand the church's identity and purpose, we have to begin with God the Father's plan to rescue sinful people through the blood of His Son and preserve them by His Spirit. As part of this glorious work, God mercifully reconciles us who were His enemies to Himself and unites us across ethnic lines as one body to bring Him glory. And when we begin to comprehend some of the dimensions of His gracious love, we are positioned to apply redemptive truth in everyday choices and relationships and thereby grow into the likeness of Jesus Christ. This is *new life in Christ.*

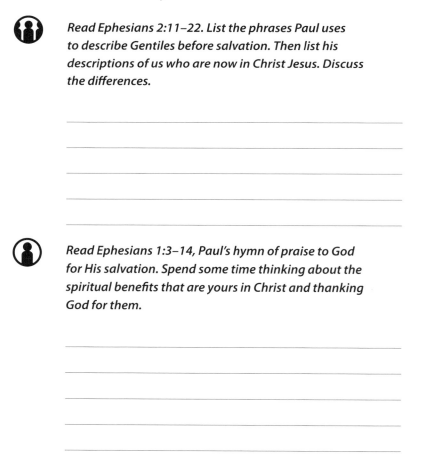

Read Ephesians 2:11–22. List the phrases Paul uses to describe Gentiles before salvation. Then list his descriptions of us who are now in Christ Jesus. Discuss the differences.

_____

_____

_____

_____

_____

Read Ephesians 1:3–14, Paul's hymn of praise to God for His salvation. Spend some time thinking about the spiritual benefits that are yours in Christ and thanking God for them.

_____

_____

_____

_____

_____

Notes

02
The Message of Ephesians

In the preceding chapter we considered the city of Ephesus, the beginning of the church there, and the purpose of Paul's letter to the churches in that area. Now our focus turns to the message of Ephesians. As in many of his writings, Paul divides this letter into two sections. In Ephesians 1–3 he explains magnificent theology. It is one of the richest sections of soteriology—the doctrine of salvation—in all the Bible. Then he builds on this theological truth with the blocks of practical application. Whereas there is only one command in the first three chapters—"remember" (2:11)—the final three chapters contain approximately forty. In light of God's glorious grace, we must walk a certain way. We have been recreated to reflect Christ.

God's Glorious Work in the Church by Christ Jesus

The first three chapters of Ephesians are a compelling account of God's glorious grace in saving the church through Christ Jesus (Eph. 3:21). It is like the Himalayas. There isn't just one impressive peak but rather an entire range of them. Paul uses the metaphor of wealth to express the splendor of God's saving work. "The riches of [God's] grace" (1:7) are an unfathomable treasure. Therefore, the only fitting responses to this grace are to give God praise and glory (1:6, 12, 14) and to exhibit by our lives how amazing God's grace is. That's why the last three chapters are Paul's exhortation to live out this new life in Christ together as the church.

One of the ways Paul describes His message of God's salvation is as the revelation of a *mystery*. The Father "made known unto us the mystery of his will" (1:9). In chapter 3 Paul expands this idea, explaining that the unveiled gospel incorporates believing Gentiles in the sweep of God's redemption (3:3–4, 9). It was Paul's divine appointment to "preach among the Gentiles the unsearchable riches of Christ" (3:8). And one of the results of this unfolding mystery is that angelic beings watch with marvel at God's wisdom displayed in the church (3:10). The dimensions and richness of our salvation are incomprehensible, even to supernatural beings. By Christ Jesus, the Father glorifies Himself *in the church* and will do so forever (3:20–21).

 Paul indicates the theme of unity in many ways, including the recurring phrase "in [or by] Christ." Locate these references in Ephesians and then discuss some of our blessings together in Christ (Eph. 1:3).

How does the church manifest "the manifold wisdom of God" (Eph. 3:10)? Why is the church so important in God's redemptive plan?

_____

_____

_____

_____

Our United Life as the Church in Christ Jesus

As amazing as the first half of Ephesians is, the letter does not end there. The truth of the gospel provides the foundation and motivation for us to live as new people in Christ.

The connection between chapters 1–3 and 4–6 is signified by the word therefore *in Ephesians 4:1. In fact, Paul uses this word several times in Ephesians 4–6 to explain the reasons for his commands. See if you can find five additional occurrences.*

_____

_____

_____

_____

Paul links together his exhortation in chapters 4–6 with the metaphor of *walking*. It is a simple picture of everyday life. It's what healthy human beings do. God brings us to life in Christ (2:6) and then prepares a life of good works for us to walk in (2:10).

We naturally want to know what this everyday conduct looks like. So Paul specifies:

1. "*Walk* worthy of the vocation wherewith ye are called" (4:1). Paul explains that God has called us to live out our identity as His church, which entails maintaining unity and growing into the maturity of Jesus Christ.
2. "Henceforth *walk* not as other Gentiles walk" (4:17). In other words, unbelievers characteristically think and act in certain ways that Christians must renounce and avoid. Instead, we pursue new habits that evidence a new identity and a renewed mind.
3. "And *walk* in love, as Christ also hath loved us, and hath given himself for us an offering and a sacrifice to God for a sweetsmelling savour" (5:2). Living out our new life in Christ means imitating His love in our relationships, rather than imitating the world's sensuality and covetousness.
4. "*Walk* as children of light" (5:8). Christians are transformed, not only from our former behavior (4:25–32) but also from our present culture. "The children of disobedience" live in darkness (5:6–7), so we must clearly distinguish ourselves from them.
5. "See then that ye *walk* circumspectly, not as fools, but as wise" (5:15). As Paul describes in the following verses, by submitting ourselves to God's Spirit we will display true wisdom in human relationships that are marked by sacrificial love and humble obedience.

This is the kind of life that evidences and enriches our unity in Christ, in whom we have a divine calling, a renewed mindset, a supernatural love, a true holiness, and spiritual wisdom.

But it is not without adversity. Living as new people in Christ brings us into direct conflict with God's archenemy, the Devil. He and his minions, "the rulers of the darkness of this world" (6:12), have schemes (6:11) and "fiery darts" (6:16) by which they intend to wound and defeat us. So the opposition we face is not simply coming from those with an alternate viewpoint. Actually, our calling as the church of Christ Jesus (4:1) entails supernatural warfare. The stakes could not be higher.

 Read Ephesians 6:10–20. What does Paul instruct us to do in order to stand in Christ's victory over our ancient foe, the Devil?

_____

_____

_____

_____

_____

Conclusion

After emphasizing the need for unity (4:1–6) and explaining how Christ has gifted His church (4:7–11), Paul summarizes how discipleship takes place. The body of Christ grows into its Head, who is Christ, by *truthing in love* (4:15). In contrast with the clever deceit of false teachers, we build one another up by living and speaking the truth we have been taught. Teaching and preaching are critical but are not an end in themselves. We must do something with God's Word by faith. Discipleship is active and involves every member of the body; discipleship is the hands-on ministry of *edifying toward maturity*.

This maturity is quite practical. Growing into the fullness of Jesus Christ (or putting on the new man) relates to all of life, which means a lot of change needs to occur (putting off the old man). What kind of change would this involve? In what areas do our minds need to be renewed? This transformation involves our speech, our work ethic, our self-control, our ministry to others, our love and forgiveness, and more! Renewed thinking leads to transformed habits as we live out our new life in Christ.

 Review Paul's five commands concerning how we walk. Choose one and read the verses that come after it. Meditate on what it would mean to live like this and pray for God to conform you in this way to Jesus Christ.

_____

_____

_____

_____

_____

Notes

03
How Then Shall We Not Walk?

EPHESIANS 4:17–19

This I say therefore, and testify in the Lord, that ye henceforth walk not as other Gentiles walk, in the vanity of their mind, having the understanding darkened, being alienated from the life of God through the ignorance that is in them, because of the blindness of their heart: who being past feeling have given themselves over unto lasciviousness, to work all uncleanness with greediness.

It is possible for believing people like us who are truly distressed by the course of this world to live lives that are so profoundly influenced by culture that Sodom is reborn in the lives of those we love the most.[1]

Sometimes the most helpful instruction is to highlight a negative example. For example, perhaps your middle school teacher drove home the importance of loyalty by telling the story of the famous American traitor Benedict Arnold. In other words, we often need direction on what *not* to do in order to understand the correct way. The Holy Spirit through Paul uses this strategy to direct us in our lives as the redeemed Church. He begins in Ephesians 4:17–19 by telling us how *not* to walk. This sobering depiction of unbelievers provides

---

[1]R. Kent Hughes, *Set Apart: Calling a Worldly Church to a Godly Life* (Wheaton: Crossway Books, 2003), 15.

a dark backdrop against which the light of a renewed life in Christ will shine. These verses begin an extended contrast that shows the transforming difference God's grace makes in the life of a believer.

EPHESIANS 4:17–18	PARAPHRASE
This I say therefore, and testify in the Lord, that ye henceforth walk not as other Gentiles walk,	I solemnly affirm this truth by Christ's own authority that you no longer behave as unsaved sinners
in the vanity of their mind,	who live according to a completely worthless mindset
having the understanding darkened,	(1) that in its moral reflection is covered in darkness
being alienated from the life of God through the ignorance that is in them, because of the blindness of their heart:	(2) that is separated in hostility from God's life because of willful ignorance and a stubborn insensibility to spiritual truth and
who being past feeling have given themselves over unto lasciviousness, to work all uncleanness with greediness.	(3) that results in a callous abandonment of moral restraint in order to practice all kinds of impurity, with greed but not satisfaction.

Note all the times in Ephesians 4:20–5:17 that words like but are used to set up a contrast. What is the significance of this pattern in this section?

Paul solemnly commands the Ephesian believers to conduct their lives in a manner that is completely different from the prevailing, corrupt lifestyle of the Gentiles (or unbelievers). Our new life in Christ demands a new lifestyle. Paul reminds us of our former meaningless condition—hardened towards God, full of darkness, and morally bankrupt—with the purpose of showing us where we came from and what we can no longer be.

First of all, **Gentiles are hardened towards God**. Their hearts are like petrified wood, impenetrable because of their stubbornness towards God. Little conviction breaks through to their hearts, because they have willfully resisted the knowledge of the truth. They have become internally calloused and can no longer feel guilt or shame for their moral sins. The root of all error and idolatry in mankind springs out of a stubborn, hardened heart towards God. Their deepest problem is not ignorance but stubbornness, "because that, when they knew God, they glorified Him not as God" (Romans 1:21).

Secondly, **Gentiles live in darkness**. Though they may be intellectually gifted, they have no spiritual light and are mentally incapacitated when it comes to knowing God (1 Cor. 1:21). Gentiles are incapable of knowing the truth, because they lack divine illumination, due to satanic bondage. "But if our gospel be hid, it is hid to them that are lost: in whom the god of this world hath blinded the minds of them which believe not, lest the light of the glorious gospel of Christ, who is the image of God, should shine unto them" (2 Cor. 4:3–4). Unbelievers are alienated from the greatest reality in the universe—God—and are therefore incapable of understanding life's purpose.

Thirdly, **Gentiles are morally bankrupt**. Because of their hardened hearts, they have thrown off God's moral standards and have abandoned themselves to self-gratification. They flaunt their sexuality in public without shame and gratify it in private without guilt. They are preoccupied with their morally corrupt appetites, which can never be satisfied. In the end the hard-hearted Gentiles are slaves to their lusts, for which they are ultimately ruined and eternally damned (Eph. 2:3; 5:5).

Lasciviousness *is an uncommon word today. It conveys an attitude that regards sex as nothing more than an unrestrained means to pleasure with no accompanying sense of responsibility.*

Ephesians 4:19 says unbelievers "have given themselves over unto lasciviousness." Look up Romans 1:24, 26, and 28. Note who gives sinners over to their sinful desires in these verses. (Paul uses the same Greek verb.) Write down the connection between Ephesians 4 and Romans 1.

_____

_____

_____

_____

Consequently, **Gentiles live meaningless lives**. Their lives are full of "vanity" (4:17). Since they do not know God, they have not discovered life's purpose. They make choices simply to satisfy their own desires or to fulfill ambitions that have no eternal meaning or value. Therefore, their lives are ultimately futile.

 Discuss the mentality of unbelievers today in the following areas:

Music

_____

_____

_____

Entertainment

_____

_____

_____

Dress

_____

_____

_____

Relationships

_____

_____

_____

As believers, we must decisively break with the old life as characterized by the Gentiles, making every attempt to ensure that our lives are free of worldly motivations and practices. Becoming a Christian means receiving a new life full of meaning, a life in Christ (2 Cor. 5:17). We are now a part of the church, the body of Christ. The moral image of God is within our hearts creating new, fresh desires to change and to become like Christ. Our testimony to the power of God in salvation is seen in the transformation that has taken place in our lives.

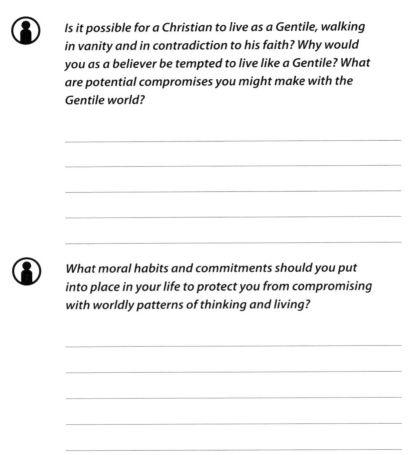

Is it possible for a Christian to live as a Gentile, walking in vanity and in contradiction to his faith? Why would you as a believer be tempted to live like a Gentile? What are potential compromises you might make with the Gentile world?

_____

_____

_____

_____

_____

What moral habits and commitments should you put into place in your life to protect you from compromising with worldly patterns of thinking and living?

_____

_____

_____

_____

_____

Notes

04
With Christ in the School of Conversion

EPHESIANS 4:20–24

But ye have not so learned Christ; if so be that ye have heard him, and have been taught by him, as the truth is in Jesus: that ye put off concerning the former conversation the old man, which is corrupt according to the deceitful lusts; and be renewed in the spirit of your mind; and that ye put on the new man, which after God is created in righteousness and true holiness.

The genuineness of our knowledge of God is revealed by whether or not we are obeying the truth that we have from his Word.[1]

Have you ever noticed how a football coach reacts after one of his players commits a personal foul against the opponent, costing his team fifteen precious yards? He doesn't usually offer a slaphappy bear hug, does he? But for coaches whose objectives transcend merely winning or showing off their temper, such penalties provide important teaching moments. And one of the understandable messages conveyed in these situations goes something like this: "You know better than that. You play for ABC University. We play disciplined football. We are different."

---

[1]David F. Wells, *God in the Whirlwind: How the Holy-love of God Reorients Our World* (Wheaton: Crossway, 2014), 173.

The grace of God changes us to live distinctly, not carelessly as if we were still lost. After reminding the Ephesians of their former lifestyle as Gentiles, Paul testifies that the believer's way of life is absolutely incompatible with the conduct of the surrounding heathen culture. Why? Paul explains that the believers must live differently because they have entered into a life-changing experience with Christ in the school of conversion.

EPHESIANS 4:20–24	PARAPHRASE
But ye have not so learned Christ;	But it was not in this worldly way that you received instruction from and about Christ,
if so be that ye have heard him, and have been taught by him, as the truth is in Jesus:	if you really heard and were instructed by Him (after all, the truth is in Jesus)
that ye put off concerning the former conversation the old man, which is corrupt according to the deceitful lusts;	(1) that at conversion you laid aside your old self with reference to your former way of life that was thoroughly corrupted by deceitful desires,
and be renewed in the spirit of your mind;	(2) and that presently you are being totally renovated in your thinking by God the Spirit,
and that ye put on the new man, which after God is created in righteousness and true holiness.	(3) and that at conversion you also clothed yourself with a new nature that is recreated according to God's image of righteousness and true holiness.

Paul uses the metaphor of a classroom to illustrate the way in which an unbeliever is converted. Using the three parallel expressions *learned*, *heard*, and *taught*, Paul refers to the basic truths the Ephesians had learned under the apostles' instruction. His curriculum was about Christ, both His life and work, but it was much more than that. To hear Paul was to hear Jesus. Christ Himself had been communicated to them through the ministry of the Holy Spirit. "But when the Comforter is come, whom I will send unto you from the Father, even the Spirit of truth, which proceedeth from the Father, he shall testify of me" (John 15:26). The Ephesians had not only learned Christ through the simple disseminating of historical facts about His life, they had actually learned Christ! Christ was not only the subject of the message but also the teacher. So what were the lessons that the Ephesians learned with Christ in the school of conversion?

Two of the most important New Testament passages concerning Jesus Christ and truth are John 1:14–18 and John 18:33–37. Write down how they help explain what Paul means in Ephesians 4:21.

———————————————————————

———————————————————————

———————————————————————

———————————————————————

———————————————————————

First of all, Paul reminds believers that when we "learned Christ," **we put off the old man**. What does Paul mean by the *old man*? Christ's mission on earth was to undo what Adam had done in the Garden of Eden. Adam's sin and disobedience affected all of humanity because of his role as the representative head of the human race. Judicially, Adam's guilt was transferred to mankind (Rom. 5:18), and as a result, his sinful nature was transmitted to all men through procreation (Ps. 51:5). Because of this, each of us is condemned by imputed guilt and controlled by an inherent sinful nature. The old man is everything mankind is in Adam.

This old man is characterized by a life that is continually corrupted by deceitful passions. Human nature is predisposed to self-centeredness, so the only choice an unbeliever can make is to sin. The lusts of the old man continually promise satisfaction through indulgence, but this is all self-deception. In reality, these desires lead to greater enslavement to sin, which corrupts the emotions, conscience, intellect, and even physical constitution. The work of Christ is to deliver us from this old man state. The old man was nailed to the cross with Christ. "Our old man is crucified with him" (Rom. 6:6). Christ's death sets us free from the bondage and power of the old sinful life. "That the body of sin might be destroyed, that henceforth we should not serve sin" (Rom. 6:6). Though the remnants of the old man (the flesh) are not eradicated from the body, they no longer have dominating control over our life. Sin's power has been broken!

The second lesson we learn is that **God has created new life within us called the new man**. This new life is rooted in the resurrection of Christ (Rom. 6:5). If believers have participated in the death of Christ, then we have surely taken part in His resurrection. What is this new life? It is a restoration of the image of God in the human soul, an image lost by Adam's disobedience but regained by Christ's obedience (Rom. 5:19). The inherent qualities of this new man are *righteousness* (a desire to do what God requires) and *holiness* (a devotion to know and love God). Therefore, change begins internally through the sanctified desires of the new life.

 Paul also mentions the old man and new man in Colossians 3. According to verses 8–10 what kind of sins

did we die to, and what kind of characteristics did we become alive to in our conversion?

_____

_____

_____

_____

_____

The Ephesians' experience in the school of conversion took place at a certain point in time. Every main verb in Ephesians 4:20–24 is in the past tense, with one exception: "And be *renewed*" (4:23). This renewal is the focus of the next chapter. When did this event occur? As the truth of the gospel is preached to sinners in the power of the Spirit who reveals Christ to them, sinners like those in the Ephesian church *put off* the old life through repentance and *put on* the new life by receiving Christ through faith. We call this entire experience *conversion*. In the 1700s, evangelist George Whitfield declared: "Before you or I can have any well-grounded, scriptural hope of being happy in a future state, there must be some great, some notable, and amazing change pass upon our souls."[2]

As believers we cannot live like Gentiles, because we have entered into a new life with Christ. Our new life brings many changes as a result of putting off our old man and putting on the new man. This experience of change continues throughout our lives, as we are continually renewed in the spirit of our minds. Sanctification is "the process whereby the Spirit of God

---

[2]George Whitefield, *The Works of the Reverend George Whitefield* (Edinburgh: Edward and Charles Dilly, 1772), 339.

takes the Word of God and changes us to become like the Son of God."[3]

Give your own personal testimony of conversion.

_____

_____

_____

_____

_____

Why should we have a confidence that we can actually change?

_____

_____

_____

_____

_____

Do you sense that you've experienced the new life? Explain.

_____

_____

_____

_____

_____

[3]Jim Berg, _Changed into His Image_ (Greenville, SC: BJU Press, 1999), 9.

Notes

05
Renewing the Mind

EPHESIANS 4:23

And be renewed in the spirit of your mind.

Right thinking about the gospel produces right living in the gospel.
It is truth, not activity, which makes Christianity distinct.
We cannot ignore the link between gospel doctrine and
gospel duty if we hope to approach genuine Christian life
and successful Christian living.[1]

Positioned between the glorious events of the old man being put off at conversion and the new man put on by the Spirit's regeneration is the fundamental process by which believers are changed into Christlikeness—the *renewing of the mind*. Paul urges believers to be continually renewed in the spirit of our minds. Before we can understand what renewal is, we must first understand what it is not.

---

[1]Michael P. V. Barrett, *Complete in Him*, (Greenville, SC: Ambassador-Emerald International, 2000), 3.

EPHESIANS 4:23	PARAPHRASE
And be renewed in the spirit of your mind.	Be progressively, internally made new (by God) in your emotions, attitudes, and reasoning.

First of all, **renewing the mind is not an experience to be separated from conversion**. Paul strategically places this verse between his explanation of the acts of putting off and putting on. The process of renewal, known also as progressive sanctification, must never be separated from the initial experience of conversion and regeneration. Though sanctification is not identical to conversion and regeneration, all three are vital parts of the whole. The initial acts of repentance and faith are followed by the process of spiritual growth and maturity and conclude with the final experience of entering into heaven in a glorified state. Any system of theology that excludes any of these aspects in its doctrine of salvation is in error.

Secondly, **renewing the mind is not just an intellectual exercise**. Bible study and Scripture memorization are not the only activities involved in the renewing of the mind. A person could spend four years in a Christian university or earn a degree from a theological seminary and yet experience little spiritual maturity. Many church members regularly sit under the faithful teaching and preaching of God's Word, but their lives reveal no apparent change. Intellectual knowledge of the Bible is obviously not equivalent to being renewed in the spirit of the mind.

Thirdly, **renewing the mind is not simply replacing old habits and establishing new ones**. An unregenerate man can make basic moral changes. The very things that Paul commands us to put off—lying, stealing, anger, corrupt communication—are actually things that could be superficially changed by unbelievers. Paul is talking about something far deeper than self-improvement or external character development. He is talking about a complete renovation of the inner person that can be accomplished only by God's Spirit.

Read Luke 11:24–26. Then think about the difference between cleaning your bedroom and renovating it. How do this passage and this illustration help us distinguish what renewing the mind truly is?

_____

_____

_____

_____

_____

What then is the renewing of the mind? First, "be renewed" is in the passive voice, meaning that God (not the Christian) is the primary agent of renewal. At regeneration, God reinstates His image, tarnished by the Fall, within the human soul. A new moral freedom and power is imparted through the indwelling presence of the Holy Spirit, enabling the believer to do the will of God and to contend against the flesh principle that remains within him. Second, "be renewed" is in the present tense, meaning that sanctification is ongoing and progressive. Renewal is therefore the continual change of life that began initially at conversion. At salvation, we were introduced to Christ through the preaching of the gospel. Christ spoke to our hearts as we heard the Word. We responded with the initial acts of repentance and faith, choosing to leave the old life of sin and entering the new life of faith. In essence, renewal is a daily living out in experience what took place in our heart at salvation. So how does this process work in our lives?

A similar phrase—"be ye transformed by the renewing of your mind"—occurs in Romans 12:2. What do we learn from Romans 12:1–2 about the challenge and motivation and effects of renewing our minds?

Renewal involves daily communion with Christ through His Word. Christ, working through His Spirit, allows us to behold His glory in the mirror of the Word (2 Cor. 3:18; 4:6). As we dwell in His presence by spending time meditating on His Word, a change begins to take place within our spirit and mind, and we develop an entirely new outlook on life. The habits of the new life flow out of this relationship that we have with Christ. This includes a change in our thinking, attitudes, choices, actions, and habits (Rom. 12:2). No area of our lives remains untouched!

Read 2 Corinthians 3:18, 4:4, and 4:6. Describe and discuss what these verses teach about spiritual transformation.

Renewal involves obedience. We as believers must continually strive to bring all our thoughts under the controlling influence of the Holy Spirit. The qualities that reflect the old, corrupt lifestyle must be put away with intense commitment as He exposes our own sinfulness. God is actively energizing His people with the power and the desire to change (Phil. 2:13). Therefore, we must submissively obey these strong promptings by putting on the actions and habits that reflect the new man. In the end the renewing of the mind entails a thorough renovation of our entire lives.

Read Philippians 3:7–10 and consider this thought: If the chief end of man is to glorify God and to enjoy Him forever, then the chief pursuit of man is to know God. What would pursuing the knowledge of God look like in the coming week?

_____

_____

_____

_____

_____

Describe your daily devotional time with God. (If this practice is a struggle, reach out to someone in your group who can encourage and help you.)

_____

_____

_____

_____

_____

In what areas do you need to pursue spiritual maturity?

_____

_____

_____

_____

_____

Notes

06
To Tell the Truth

EPHESIANS 4:25

Wherefore putting away lying, speak every man truth with his
neighbour: for we are members one of another.

Fellowship is built on trust, and trust is built on truth.
So falsehood undermines fellowship, while truth strengthens it.[1]

Companies typically depend on customer satisfaction. Miscommunication about a purchase or a warranty or a service can easily result in dissatisfaction. But when a prominent company like Toyota is exposed for ignoring and covering up problems, the effects can be disastrous.[2] Mistakes are one thing. Deceit is another.

In Ephesians 4:25–32, Paul exhorts believers to change our behavior in five different areas of conduct, each having a direct effect on our personal relationships with each other. Paul

---

[1]John R. W. Stott, *The Message of Ephesians*, The Bible Speaks Today (Downers Grove: Inter-Varsity Press, 1979), 185.

[2]Brian Ross et al, "Toyota to Pay $1.2B for Hiding Deadly 'Unintended Acceleration'," abcnews.go.com, March 19, 2014.

follows a three-fold pattern in each section: a negative prohibition, a positive exhortation, and a theological motive behind the command. The first realm of change that distinguishes a believer is that he speaks the truth. Truthful communication is important to a profitable company. But that temporal implication pales in comparison with the significance of truth in the church.

EPHESIANS 4:25	PARAPHRASE
Wherefore putting away lying,	For this reason, since you have laid aside deceitfulness like dirty clothes,
speak every man truth with his neighbour:	every believer must speak truth with fellow members of his Christian community,
for we are members one of another.	for we are together parts of Christ's body.

When a sinner is converted, his communication is transformed. Essentially, he stops lying and starts telling the truth. In the beginning, God's truth was *contradicted*—"ye shall not surely die"—and *misrepresented*—"you shall be as gods"—by Satan in the Garden of Eden (Gen. 3:1–5). Christ reveals the deceitful character of the devil: "Ye are of your father the devil, and the lusts of your father ye will do. He was a murderer from the beginning, and abode not in the truth, because there is no truth in him. When he speaketh a lie, he speaketh of his own: for he is a liar, and the father of it" (John 8:44). The root of humanity's primal sin was Adam's belief in Satan's lies. Everyone born since Adam bears the same inherent, fallen, deceitful nature. "The wicked are estranged from the womb: they go astray as soon as they be born, speaking lies" (Ps. 58:3). All falsehood is rooted in the fallen nature of the old man.

During the initial act of conversion, a sinner fully embraces the truth as found in God's Word. Repentance is *confessing* the truth that God declares about us—that we are sinners in need of a Savior. Faith involves *believing* "the truth [that] is in Jesus" (Eph. 4:21), that He is the Revelation of God and the Redeemer of men. We forsake the former life of idolatry (1 Thess. 1:9) and embrace the new life that is created in "righteousness and true holiness" (Eph. 4:24). From the very beginning of the Christian life, believers have put away the old garments of dishonesty and have put on the new wardrobe of truth.

After conversion believers should, as a result of daily renewal, communicate honestly with each other. Paul refers to us as the body of Christ (Eph. 5:30), since we are now members of a new humanity. If we are dishonest with one another, the body will begin to malfunction. The image of the body illustrates how important telling the truth is. Envision what would happen if our eyes did not communicate properly with our brain, which in turn did not communicate honestly with our feet while walking near a dangerous precipice. **The body of Christ can function well only when all of the members communicate honestly with one another**.

Many offenses between Christian brothers and sisters are rooted in some form of falsehood, such as:

lying—an intentionally false statement

contradictions—a combination of statements, ideas, or features of a situation that do not match one another

misrepresentation—a misleading statement

insinuation—unpleasant hints or suggestions of something in an indirect and unpleasant way

exaggeration—representing something as being larger/greater/better/worse than it really is

evasion—avoiding a direct answer to a question

silence—the avoidance of mentioning or discussing something

Paul stresses the importance of putting away lying because of its damaging effects on the body of believers. God does not look kindly on believers who lie to one another. Just ask Ananias and Sapphira! (Acts 5:1–11)

Read Acts 5:1–11. What do we learn from this account about lying and God's response to it?

_____

_____

_____

_____

Honesty is also crucial as a testimony to unbelievers. A quick way to lose effectiveness as a witness is to be found dishonest. Since the world waits for any excuse to reject Christ, Christians cannot be a stumbling block to unbelievers through their dishonesty.

Because honesty is central to who and what we are as believers, we must ask ourselves some questions.

- Are we candid with each other, or do we hide the truth because of fear?
- Do we become defensive when things about our life are truthfully pointed out or exposed?
- Do we mask our insecurity and pride by blaming others?
- Do we create bigger problems because of exaggeration?

- Do we make slanderous insinuations, discrediting the reputations of others?

How refreshing to walk with people who are totally honest with one another and are not afraid to be transparent concerning their own humanity. As we put on truth, let us put it on as a part of our new life in Christ.

Why is it so important that we speak the truth to one another in a community of believers?

_____

_____

_____

_____

_____

In what common ways are you or your peers tempted to be dishonest? What wrong motives prompt us to deceive others?

_____

_____

_____

_____

_____

What elements of dishonesty are you prone to committing? (See the list above.)

_____

_____

_____

_____

_____

Has there been a recent incident of dishonesty that you need to put off by confessing and making it right? What are the first steps you need to take to make it right?

_____

_____

_____

_____

_____

Notes

07
Be Angry, but Don't Sin

EPHESIANS 4:26–27

Be ye angry, and sin not: let not the sun go down upon your wrath: neither give place to the devil.

To dissolve our sinful emotions, we must believe that God is absolutely sovereign in all the affairs of our lives (both the 'good' and the 'bad') and that all the words and actions of other people that tempt us to anger are somehow included in His wise and good purposes to make us more like Jesus.[1]

What happens when you are running late for an important appointment and you get stuck in traffic? What if you dump coffee on your pants or your phone battery dies? Most of us find ourselves in situations when anger of some sort—impatience, frustration, irritation, bitterness—spills or spews out. But is anger always wrong? What about the fire that arises in your soul when you hear of a child abused, or dozens

---

[1] Jerry Bridges, *Respectable Sins: Confronting the Sins We Tolerate* (Colorado Springs: NavPress, 2007), 126.

of people killed by a terrorist, or a scam that takes advantage of unsuspecting senior citizens?

"Be angry!" Paul's imperative, which at first may seem confusing, is a divine command. But is he referring to unlimited or unrestricted anger? In these two verses, Paul gives four direct commands concerning the way believers should handle anger.

EPHESIANS 4:26–27	PARAPHRASE
Be ye angry,	Be enraged over sin,
and sin not:	but don't sin in your anger.
let not the sun go down upon your wrath:	Don't let angry irritation go unchecked,
neither give place to the devil.	and don't provide an opening for the slanderer.

First of all, **Paul acknowledges that situations *will* occur in which God's people should experience anger.** Tensions *will* arise between believers because of various issues, such as negligence, ignorance, stubbornness, and inconsistency. Christ Himself was angered over the hardness of human hearts (Mark 3:5). Included in this allowance to be angry are the corruption and injustices believers face every day in this fallen world. Blatant evil within society should incite the anger of believers and motivate us to take a stand for righteousness. Because of evil in the world, many of God's people have responded by starting great ministries: crisis pregnancy centers, orphanages, addiction programs, Christian schools, relief organizations, and mission societies. Paul commands us to be angry for a righteous cause.

Secondly, **Paul quickly restricts anger—"and sin not" (Eph. 4:26).** Being angry and yet not sinning requires that a believer be angry at *nothing but sin*. Paul is citing an Old Testament text, "Stand in awe, and sin not" (Ps. 4:4). The Psalmist's experience with the vanity and lies of his enemies caused him great distress. The command is to trust God with the unfairness of life and not to indulge in anger. The jump from initial feelings of anger to sin is not very far. Anger can degenerate very rapidly into emotional outbursts, irritable attitudes (manifested in looks and words), or resentment and bitterness. Indulging in anger seriously hinders the unity of the body of believers and the joy they have in their relationships with one another.

 Read Romans 12:14–21. How do Paul's commands in this passage help us understand what it looks like to avoid sinful anger?

_____

_____

_____

_____

Thirdly, **Paul places a time limit on anger as a safeguard.** He is not telling us to dispense with our anger as we watch the sun set in the evening. His proverbial saying implies that anger should be dealt with promptly. The very nature of anger makes it extremely hard to control, and it can easily turn, therefore, into something that is unrighteous. "Let every man be . . . slow to wrath: for the wrath of man worketh not the righteousness of God" (James 1:19–20). The two words in this passage, *anger* and *wrath,* reveal the primary issue at hand. Righteous anger *can* begin as a permissible attitude. However, it can fester, leading to unrighteous indignation. Therefore, a good rule for sanctified living is, "Don't go to bed mad."

Contrast righteous anger with unrighteous anger.

_____

_____

_____

_____

_____

*What are some biblical truths that will help us deal
quickly with anger?*

_____

_____

_____

_____

Finally, **Paul unveils a warning of immense proportion.** He
urges us to give *no* "place to the devil" (Eph. 4:27). Satan uses
anger as a base of operation to exert his influence over us.
Devil means *slanderer*, one who makes false statements with
the intent to damage the reputation of another. This is a prime
example of spiritual warfare. The devil's intent is to provoke
us to distrust one another. Satan wrestles with believers in the
moral sphere seeking to gain a foothold through uncontrolled
anger. He aims to create a spirit of distrust within the church,
ultimately dividing the fellowship and disrupting the unity
created by the Spirit (Eph. 4:3).

God *does* permit His people, who live in a fallen world of im-
perfections and evil, to "be angry." However, keeping righteous
anger pure is very difficult. Since our adversary, the devil, is an
opportunist, we must vigilantly deny him the opportunity to
work his evil through our unrestrained anger. In all situations,

we are to commit ourselves to God, who alone deals with injustice in a righteous manner: "Dearly beloved, avenge not yourselves . . . for it is written, Vengeance is mine; I will repay, saith the Lord" (Rom. 12:19).

 Think of a time when the Devil has taken advantage of your anger. What was the "opening" that he exploited? What truth can you apply to seal off that opening?

_____

_____

_____

_____

_____

For further help with anger, see David Powlison, *Good and Angry: Redeeming Anger, Irritation, Complaining, and Bitterness* (Greensboro, NC: New Growth Press, 2016).

Notes

08
Stealing, Working, Giving

EPHESIANS 4:28

Let him that stole steal no more: but rather let him labour, working with his hands the thing which is good, that he may have to give to him that needeth.

No man liveth for himself; and no man should labour for himself alone, but with the definite object to be able to assist others.[1]

Wealth is a prominent topic in Jesus' own teaching in the Gospels. Christ extols those, like the Good Samaritan, who give of their possessions to help people in need (Luke 10:33–37). He honors the widow who gave her only mite (Mark 12:42–44). The Gospel writer records the monetary effect of Zacchaeus's conversion (Luke 19:8). On the other hand, Jesus condemns the rich man who hoarded his riches (Luke 12:15–20), and He throws the moneychangers out of the temple (Matt. 21:12). In other words, money is only temporal, but what we do with it on earth is eternally significant.

---

[1]Charles Hodge, *A Commentary on Ephesians*, The Geneva Series of Commentaries (Edinburgh: Banner of Truth Trust, 1964), 198.

In New Testament times, many of the converts to Christianity were slaves, common day-laborers, and skilled tradesmen. Life was hard and the pay was low (or nothing at all), especially if someone owned you! Stealing was a norm of pagan society as people tried to survive from day to day. However, Paul reveals that the new life in Christ makes stealing intolerable for believers. Instead, believers should work hard, so that we may have the joy of giving to those in need.

EPHESIANS 4:28	PARAPHRASE
Let him that stole steal no more:	The thief must steal no longer
but rather let him labour,	but instead labor diligently,
working with his hands the thing which is good,	accomplishing with his own hands what is good
that he may have to give to him that needeth.	in order to have something to share with those in need.

Paul begins with a negative directive to the thief: stop stealing! Thievery denies God as the One who meets the needs of His people (Heb. 13:5–6); theft totally disrupts the unity, trust, and fellowship of the Christian community. The new, recreated image of God's righteousness in the life of believers demands that we put away stealing. Not only was theft a sin in the Old Testament (Ex. 20:15; Lev. 19:11; Deut. 5:19), but Paul clearly taught elsewhere in the New Testament that loving one's neighbor means not stealing from them (Rom. 13:9). We see an example in the life of Zacchaeus the tax collector, who, when he received Christ, was willing to give half of his goods to the poor and repay fourfold those whom he had robbed (Luke 19:8). In contrast is the example of Judas Iscariot, who hypocritically implied that he cared for the poor yet was later discovered to be a thief (John 12:6). Life made new in Christ requires that stealing be stopped so that the body of believers can achieve a higher level of trust and respect.

Describe ways in which we may be tempted to steal. Think of both illegal and (technically) legal ways.

Paul follows with a positive command that believers work with their hands. Prior to conversion, the lazy man used theft to make a living. That which *was* obtained with little effort must *now* be gained by diligent labor. Paul had made his living by working with his hands as a tentmaker, and so he exhorts his congregations to work with their hands as well (1 Thess. 4:11; 2 Thess. 3:8–9). Our labor should be for the mutual benefit and blessing of all people while providing for the needs of our own lives and families in an honest manner.

Paul ends by explaining one of the primary benefits of work for the believer: that "he may have to give to him that need-eth" (Eph. 4:28). In Acts 20:35 Paul reminds the Ephesian elders of his own lifestyle while he was with them: "I have shewed you all things, how that so labouring ye ought to support the weak, and to remember the words of the Lord Jesus, how he said, It is more blessed to give than to receive." The purpose of work is not the acquisition of wealth for the fulfillment of the American Dream, but the opportunity to experience the joy of giving to others (1 Tim. 6:17–18). This is Christlikeness. "For ye know the grace of our Lord Jesus Christ, that, though he was rich, yet for your sakes he became poor, that ye through his poverty might be rich" (2 Cor. 8:9).

Read 2 Corinthians 8:1–15. What does this passage teach about Christian giving? (For further instruction, study the rest of 2 Corinthians 8–9.)

_____

_____

_____

_____

Consider the impact on the church if God's people refused to take shortcuts, worked hard, and gave generously. An atmosphere of honesty and mutual trust and respect would permeate everything we do, and progress would take place because of diligent work. God's work would go forward through His people's support of the needs of the gospel.

How does a Christian differ from an unsaved sinner in his ultimate purpose of work?

_____

_____

_____

_____

C. S. Lewis wrote, "I am afraid the only safe rule is to give more than we can spare. In other words, if our expenditure on comforts, luxuries, amusements, etc., is up to the standard common among those with the

same income as our own, we are probably giving away too little. If our charities do not at all pinch or hamper us, I should say they are too small. There ought to be things we should like to do and cannot do because our charities expenditure excludes them."[2]

What would it look like for you to embrace Lewis's honest application of Scripture's teaching?

_____

_____

_____

_____

_____

In light of Acts 20:35, is it your tendency to give or to receive? Do you find giving to be truly blessed? Consider how you could give your time, money, or talents in one way this week in order to demonstrate Christ's love to someone else.

_____

_____

_____

_____

_____

---

[2]C. S. Lewis, *Mere Christianity* (New York: HarperCollins, 1980), 116–17.

Notes

09
Christian Communication and the Holy Spirit

EPHESIANS 4:29–30

Let no corrupt communication proceed out of your mouth, but that which is good to the use of edifying, that it may minister grace unto the hearers. And grieve not the holy Spirit of God, whereby ye are sealed unto the day of redemption.

Word problems reveal heart problems. The people and situations around us do not make us say what we say; they are only the occasion for our hearts to reveal themselves in word.[1]

Power tools are wonderful modern inventions. Whether you're using a chainsaw to cut down a dead tree, a washing machine to clean your clothes, or an impact driver to put together a Ping-Pong table, the efficiency and comparative ease of power tools make everyday life better. But things can also go terribly wrong. Broken equipment, carelessness, and accidents quickly turn amazing tools into frustrating problems or even dangerous weapons.

---

[1]Paul David Tripp, *War of Words: Getting to the Heart of Your Communication Struggles* (Phillipsburg, NJ: P&R Publishing Co., 2000), 55.

One of the most powerful tools that God has given to influence one another in the church is the tongue. We can use good words to minister grace to fellow believers, or we can grieve the Holy Spirit with evil words. Paul presents two prohibitions concerning the way we communicate. First of all, our words must not be harmful; secondly, the Holy Spirit must not be grieved. Instead, we are exhorted to speak words that dispense grace to build up the church.

EPHESIANS 4:29–30	PARAPHRASE
Let no corrupt communication proceed out of your mouth,	Make sure no rotten speech pours out of your mouth,
but that which is good to the use of edifying,	but instead speak profitable words that build up those in need,
that it may minister grace unto the hearers.	in order to minister grace to those who hear you.
And grieve not the holy Spirit of God,	And stop grieving the Holy Spirit of God
whereby ye are sealed unto the day of redemption.	by whom you are sealed until the day when Jesus' ransom releases you from sin's presence.

Paul's first prohibition allows no room for corrupt communication. Sinful speech does more to harm the communal life of the church than all the sins previously mentioned in this passage. Words that are profane, slanderous, offensive, critical, and divisive will set a negative temperature among believers; therefore, God calls us to a serious restraint of the tongue (James 3:2). We can permit nothing to proceed from our mouths that harms the unity of the church.

What kind of communication is corrupt? What motivation lies behind fleshly words?

_____

_____

_____

_____

_____

In Matthew 12:36–37 Jesus says, "But I say unto you, That every idle word that men shall speak, they shall give account thereof in the day of judgment. For by thy words thou shalt be justified, and by thy words thou shalt be condemned." What does this passage teach about the importance of our words?

_____

_____

_____

_____

Behind this severe restriction lies a deeply spiritual motive going to the very heart of the new man—the permanent residence of the Holy Spirit who indwells the believer. Paul has already stated that the Ephesians were sealed with the Spirit (Eph. 1:13), a stamping of God's ownership on us and a securing of our future salvation. The Spirit will dwell in us until glory, so our words and attitudes can bring Him great sorrow. The Spirit of God is never indifferent; we live either grieving or not grieving the Spirit. God can be emotionally disappointed, disturbed, or distressed with His people! When the Spirit is grieved, our inner life is affected with an absence of the manifestation of God's love, joy and peace. We must keep an attitude of reverence towards the person of the Holy Spirit and avoid all words that would grieve Him. If He is grieved, then His people will lack His blessing.

Instead, **Paul reveals that believers have the awesome privilege of becoming dispensers of God's grace.** As co-laborers with God's Spirit, we may take part in the sanctifying process of other believers. Therefore, we must choose words carefully and speak truthfully. Paul has already stated that speaking the truth is one of the first characteristics of the new life. First of all, truth must be spoken with love, a primary agent to build up the church (Eph. 4:15). If motivated by personal frustration, our lashing out with truth cannot do the hearer good. Secondly, we must speak truth at an appropriate time (Prov. 25:11). Prayer and careful forethought should be given before speaking, so that what we say can have the greatest benefit.

We must all exercise caution when speaking with one another. Consider the times that we cause pain and sorrow to the Holy Spirit by the things that we say to each other. How many ministries lack God's blessing primarily because of believers' speech? How much growth could take place if we were communicating grace through our choice of words? Before speaking we must ask ourselves: Is this true? Can I say it in love? Is this the appropriate time? In this way we can bless one another and please the Holy Spirit.

 List five ways in which we can communicate gracious words.

_____

_____

_____

Is the Spirit grieved with the words you speak personally? Are there sins of the tongue you need to repent of and forsake?

_____

_____

_____

_____

_____

Think about and pray for two relationships in which you can turn bad speech into an opportunity to minister God's grace.

_____

_____

_____

_____

_____

Notes